CONTENTS

INTRODUCTION

From the outside, our houses and streets today don't look that different from how they did in 1945. There have been many changes, however. Homes are much more comfortable now and their number has almost doubled in just 60 years.

MORE NEEDED!

During World War II (1939-45), bombing damaged one third of all the houses in Britain and left over 500,000 unfit to live in. There was a serious shortage of homes. Millions of houses have been built since then – up to 300,000 a year – but still we don't have enough to meet the demand.

There are two reasons for this. Firstly, the population of Britain has grown from 47 million to over 60 million – and all the extra people need somewhere to live. Secondly, today most people want a place of their own. Young adults like to leave home, for example rather than live with their parents as people had done in the past.

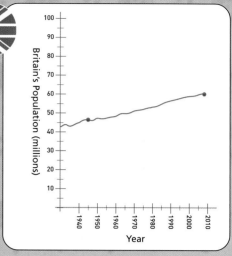

▲ A graph showing how Britain's population has soared since World War II.

▲ Children sit outside a ruined house during the Blitz in 1940. After World War II ended, lots of new houses had to be built to replace destroyed homes.

IMPROVING OUR HOUSING

In 1945, about 30 per cent of homes had no electricity and open coal fires were normal for heating. Far worse, around a million homes were thought to be unfit for people to live in them.

Things began to change quickly after 1945. The government paid councils to clear away the slums

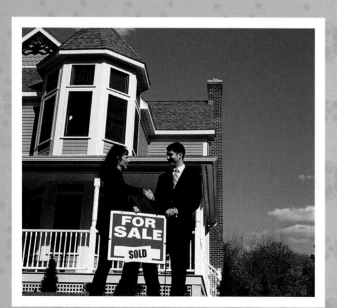

◀ In Britain today, most people want to own their own home at some time in their life.

BRITAIN SINCE WORLD WAR II

Home Life

STEWART ROSS

FRANKLIN WATTS

LONDON • SYDNEY

First published in 2007 by
Franklin Watts
338 Euston Road
London NW1 3BH

Franklin Watts Australia
Level 17/207 Kent Street
Sydney NSW 2000
Copyright © Franklin Watts 2007

Editor: Jeremy Smith
Art director: Jonathan Hair
Design: Jason Anscomb
Picture researcher: Sophie Hartley

Picture credits: Advertising Archives: 11. Alamy: 18t, 19, 22b,
23t, 24b. Bob Jones Photography/Alamy: 16. Corbis: 6t, 15t, 13t.
Easyjet: 25t. Getty images: 10t, 17, 20, 22t, 24t, 26t. Sally and
Richard Greenhill/Alamy: 24b. istockphoto: 6b, 7, 9b, 10b, 12,
18b, 21, 25b, Photofusion Picture Library/Alamy: 15b, 23b,
popperfoto.com. 8 tr. Ben Ramos/Alamy. 8tl. Time Life
Pictures/Getty Images: 9t. VIEW Pictures Ltd/Alamy: 8b.

Dewey Classification: 941.2

ISBN: 978 0 7496 7611 7

Printed in China

Franklin Watts is a division of Hachette Children's Books, an
Hachette Livre UK company.

In 1980 Britain's Prime Minister Margaret Thatcher introduced a law allowing people to buy their council houses. Over a million people took advantage of this ruling. In 1945, most homes were rented; nowadays the majority are owned by their occupiers.

and build new homes. Even so, only 35 years ago as many as one in every eight homes did not have their own bathroom.

POOR QUALITY

Some of the houses built quickly in the 1950s and 60s were badly designed and of poor quality. This was particularly true of "tower blocks" of flats which had no gardens and nowhere for children to play. By the 21st century some of these buildings had almost become ghettos, grim buildings that were almost cut off from the outside world.

"Dee Park (Reading) is typical of the housing estates built in the 1960s, poor quality housing blocks confusingly arranged ... More traditional semi-detached homes are scattered within the maze of alleyways and neglected communal spaces ... Several flats were demolished some time ago due to their poor condition."

The verdict of the Glass House Charity, a national charity offering design advice to communities all over Britain.

1946
First prefabricated homes ('prefabs') put up.

New Towns Act allows the government to plan new towns and cities.

1950
Corby in Northamptonshire is declared a new town.

1967
Work begins on the new city of Milton Keynes.

1980
Right to Buy council houses introduced.

1980s
Docklands area of London rebuilt.

2006
Britain's population reaches 60 million.

▼ A tower block dating from the 1960s in Notting Hill, London. Buildings like these have been criticised for their poor construction and for not generating the feel of a proper community.

THEN AND NOW

Only 60 years ago, many homes did not have an inside toilet. Families either shared one or used the privy – a non-flushing toilet in an outside shed.

FIXTURES AND FITTINGS

Although the type of rooms in our homes have not changed much since 1945, their appearance has altered dramatically. This is because we have become more wealthy, new materials have become available, and our tastes have also changed.

▲ A photograph of a kitchen from 1968. It features a built-in cooker and a separate hob.

▲ A kitchen dating from 2006, with expensive flooring and an "island" unit in the centre.

KITCHENS AND BATHROOMS

Modern kitchens are not the same as those of 1945. After World War II, work surfaces were wooden and sinks were made from porcelain. From the 1960s, fitted kitchens were introduced, with hard plastic work surfaces and an array of matching cupboards. Lights changed too, from a single gas or electric lamp to ceiling spotlights.

By 1965, most homes had a bathroom with an enamel bath and linoleum on the floor. Hot water was often provided by a gas or electric boiler on the wall. Tiles became the trendy decoration in the 1960s, usually in colours that are no longer fashionable. Until the 1970s, for most people taking a bath was a special and expensive event that happened perhaps once or twice a week.

READY TO RELAX

Elsewhere in the house, the biggest changes came from greater wealth. More children had their own bedroom. By the 1990s, most homes had fitted carpets – then laminate and wooden floors became all the rage.

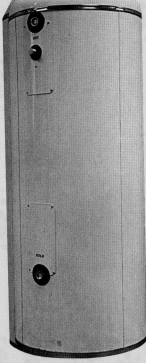

▶ A water boiler dating from the 1950s.

BUZZ BOX

The British used to think double glazing was only for very cold countries. Not any longer. All new houses and many older ones now have double-glazed windows for better insulation.

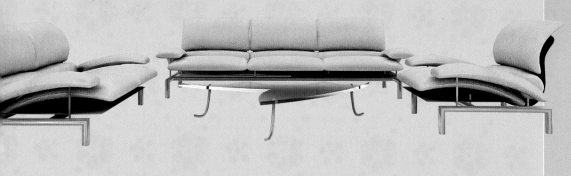

▲ A modern three piece suite, with a sofa and two matching chairs

Another big change was the spread of the three piece suite (matching sofa and two comfy chairs), which few homes had in 1945 but which most have today. Gradually, throughout the house, manufactured materials, like plastics, have become as popular as natural ones like wood and wool.

LIGHTEN UP

In 1945 homes in remote areas did not have electricity, so they had to be lit by gas or candles. By the 1980s, just about all homes had electric lights. Single bulbs were replaced by fancy spotlights. In the 21st century, new types of light bulb were introduced in an effort to save energy. Some of these can last more than five years.

▲ A new energy-saving light bulb that lasts for up to six years and uses far less electricity.

> **❝** *I remember when the electricity was switched on at home for the first time – in around 1961. Amazing! Light with the flick of a switch! Then Dad began to buy all kinds of things, like an electric kettle, a toaster and such like. Everything changed.* **❞**
>
> **Charlie Henderson remembers his childhood in the 1960s**

THEN AND NOW

We wash much more regularly than we did in 1945. Since the 1980s, we prefer taking showers to baths because they are quicker and use less water.

TIMELINE

1945
About 40 per cent of all household waste is dust and ashes from open fires.

1950s
Most homes now have indoor toilets.

1960s
Fitted kitchens and carpets widespread.

1968
Double glazing appearing in Britain.

1970
Conservatories become fashionable.

1990s
Laminate floors fashionable.

1993
All new toilets have to be water efficient.

1995
Energy-saving light bulbs first appear.

2006
Water meters compulsory for some homes in south-east England.

In 1946, housework could literally take all day, but now our homes have many "labour saving" devices. These allow us to do in just a few minutes jobs that used to take all day.

WASH DAY

In 1945, the household's washing was usually done on a particular day and normally by a woman. Monday was the popular wash day. Clothes were washed by hand. Then they were squeezed through a mangle and hung out to dry on an outside line or in front of the fire.

In the 1960s, better-off families could afford twin-tub washing machines. Others still did their washing by hand or took it to the laundrette. In the 1970s and 80s, front-loading washing machines and tumble-driers appeared and by 2000 they were common in most households.

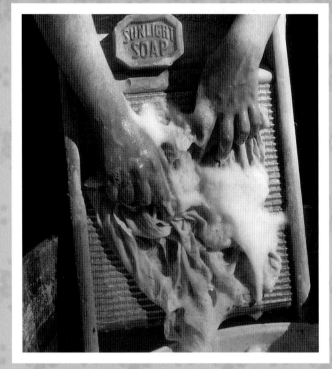

▲ A washboard was used during wash day to scrub clothes clean on.

HOUSEWORK

Many other gadgets appeared to make our lives easier and increase our leisure time. Food was kept fresh in fridges and freezers. This meant shopping could be done once a week. In the past, people had to shop every day to ensure food didn't go off. Cool cupboards called larders were used, but these could only keep food fresh for short periods of time.

◄ New inventions such as dishwashers became a feature of many homes in the 1980s.

BUZZ BOX

We still use the word "mangle" but sometimes forget where it comes from. A mangle had two rollers turned by a handle. After washing, clothes were squashed between the rollers to squeeze out water and allow the clothes to dry quicker.

Dishwashers became common in the 1980s and 90s, taking away the chore of washing up. Vacuum cleaners speeded up the once tough process of cleaning. All in all, housework took up less time. This meant that most adults had more free time to devote to other things.

MORE LEISURE

Labour-saving devices meant housework took up fewer hours. As a result, all adults, especially women, had more free time than they had enjoyed in the past. Having fewer children gave women more time, too (see pages 18-19). Many women used their freedom to take on paid work. This meant they had more money to spend, but not much more leisure time than before!

THEN AND NOW

Although vacuum cleaners were around in 1945, very few people could afford one, and they were considered a luxury. Today, nearly 100 per cent of homes have these devices.

" *Storing food never seemed to be a problem, even though they did not have a fridge. They shopped daily and therefore food kept fresh. The milkman delivered milk twice a day and non-perishable food was kept in a pantry.* "

Mary Johnson, talking about life growing up in the 1940s.

◀ A woman demonstrates the latest model of vacuum cleaner in a 1960s advert. The advert claims this invention will give her more free time.

TIMELINE

1950
Refrigerators becoming commonplace in British homes.

1951
Automatic washing machines on sale.

1955
Microwave ovens first appear.

1974
Food processors first on sale.

1980s
Dishwashers found in many homes. Ceramic hobs becoming popular.

1990
First bagless vacuum cleaner on sale.

1996
Breadmakers on sale in UK.

In 1951, the average wage for a man was £8.30 a week. In 2003, the average child's pocket money was £5.79 a week. Even though prices have risen steeply – a Mars bar cost 2p in the 1950s compared to 35p today – over the last 60 years Britain has become much, much wealthier.

GETTING AND SPENDING

We talk of Britain becoming an "affluent society" over the last 60 years. Citizens are often called "consumers" and we are urged to earn and spend as much as we can. Most people have bank accounts, and credit cards make it easy to borrow money. Car ownership is a good example of our rising affluence. In 1950, there were two million cars in use; in 1964, eight million; and in 2001, 25 million.

After World War II, most workers could expect no more than two weeks' holiday a year. Today all full-time workers are allowed at least four weeks' annual paid holiday.

▲ From the 1980s onwards, many people used credit cards to buy things, borrowing money rather than saving up in advance.

Wealth did not rise steadily. Sometimes, as in the 1970s, prices rose faster than pay. This "inflation" made life very hard for those, such as the elderly, who could not earn more. Then, during the 1980s, many old, unprofitable industries like coalmining were closed down. Over three million people became unemployed.

MEGA-RICH...

Until the 1980s, the gap between the richest and the poorest was closing.

Then it widened again. A new group of mega-rich appeared: superstar footballers earning thousands of pound a week, millionaire business people in the City of London, and other "celebrities".

❝*Our office was filled with young men in shirt-sleeves, talking on the phone and making deals. They earned more in a year than their parents had done in a lifetime.*❞

Andrew Starling in a personal interview with the author, 1994

Magazines examined every detail of their lifestyle. Advertisements, newspaper articles and TV programmes made people feel that this was the way we should all want to live.

... AND STILL POOR

But most people stood no chance of living like the super-rich. By the 1990s, a large number – perhaps 15 per cent of the population – remained trapped in poverty. These families were sometimes called an "underclass". Life for the men, women and children of this group, who often had a poor diet and bad housing, was tough and opportunities were limited.

▲ By the 1980s, traders at the London Stock Exchange were earning salaries that dwarfed the average yearly wage.

▼ While some parts of British society became richer, others got much poorer, leading to social problems in some cases. Many young people with no money had little to do with their free time and some got into trouble with the law as a result.

The last 60 years have seen big changes in our eating habits. We eat more, and much of our food is processed rather than home-made. Formal meal times are less common. We snack or eat while doing other things, like watching TV.

HOME MADE

In the 1940s and 50s, preparing meals often took several hours and certain ingredients were still rationed. Perishable foods, such as vegetables, milk, bread and meat were usually bought daily and used immediately. A typical family meal, taken with the parents and children sitting round the table, was nearly always the same: meat, potatoes and vegetables.

From the mid-50s, things began to change. Frozen and convenience foods (ready-meals, see page 15) became common, making cooking quicker and easier. Exotic foods such as avocado pears were flown in from overseas, meaning that many fruits and vegetables could be found all the year round.

> 66 *Meal times were sacrosanct. We ... sat round the table, which always sported a tablecloth. Good manners were encouraged and no one left the table until everyone had finished. I remember lots of stews – with varying amounts of meat – and lots of carrots and cabbage.* 99
>
> **Anonymous memories of meal times in the late 1940s, published on 15 November 2005 on the BBC website (www.bbc.co.uk)**

EATING OUT

In the 1950s, most families never went out for a meal at a restaurant. Fish and chips wrapped in newspaper was a weekend treat. This began to change in the 1960s as the nation became wealthier. Fast food outlets sprang up in every town and the British developed a passion for curries thanks to migrants from Asia (see pages 22-23). All kinds of different restaurants opened up, serving delicious meals and wines from all

MINISTRY OF FOOD

OFFICIAL PAID

POINTS COUPON BOOK

HOLDER'S NAME AND REGISTERED ADDRESS

Surname *Watts*

Other Names *Leslie S*

Address *15 Sunnymount Rd*
West Norwood S.E.27

If found, please return to

NATIONAL REGISTRATION NO.

ANQG. 256 1

FOOD OFFICE.

Issued by

AREA FOOD OFFICE,
PUBLIC LIBRARY,
MAGDALEN RD., S.W.18

L.86.   R.B.10

◄ For a few years after the war, food was rationed and people's diets were restricted.

BUZZ BOX

McDonald's opened their first British restaurant in Woolwich in 1974. Thirty years later, there were some 1,200 McDonald's spread all over the country.

◀ The growth of the fast food industry has contributed to problems such as obesity in British society.

over the world. Many people ate out at least once a week as a treat.

RESULTS AND REACTIONS

Two results of the food revolution were worrying. Firstly, there was a rapid rise in the number of overweight people due to a poor diet and a lack of exercise. Many of these people had health problems. Secondly, people began to eat separately rather than as a family, partly because of the introduction of "ready-meals" (pre-prepared dishes that could be cooked quickly in the microwave). As a result, families could split up into just individuals sharing a house.

In the 2000s, some experts tried to change Britons' eating habits. TV chefs made good cooking fashionable again and families were encouraged to sit down to healthy meals together. Fresh and organic foods, some sold straight from the farm, became more popular.

▲ Organic foods came into fashion from the beginning of the 21st century.

TIMELINE

1946
Bread rationed by the government.

1955
Microwave ovens first appear.

1956
First TV dinner sold.

1964
Supermarkets spreading.

1974
Britain's first McDonald's opens.

1985
Alcohol units introduced.
The maximum recommended intake for men was 3-4 units a day and 2-3 for women.

2005
Fears raised of an "obesity epidemic".

THEN AND NOW

Because of our diet, we have got a lot bigger since 1945. The average woman's waistline has increased by more than 15 cm since the end of the war.

FAMILIES

During World War II, because life was so hard, the British people had no choice but to share and work together. In the years that followed, a new importance was given to the individual. But "doing one's own thing" made family life more difficult.

RELATIONSHIPS

One of the biggest changes in society over the last 60 years has been what we see as "normal". In the 1940s and 50s, men and women normally got married, had children and stayed married. Homosexuality, divorce and having a child without being married were seen as unusual, even wrong. Until 1967, being gay was against the law.

Gradually, attitudes and behaviour changed. The number of mothers who were not married rose from around 5 per cent in the 1940s to 42 per cent in 2006. Britain's divorce rate rose to the highest in Europe. In 2005, gay couples were allowed to register their relationship like a marriage. Society had changed dramatically.

> *"My parents got divorced in the early 1970s. Some of my mum's friends refused to talk to her after that. They said she was a 'wicked woman' who should have stayed married to my father whatever!"*
>
> Richie Cooke, personal interview with author, 2006

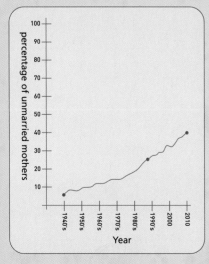

▲ A graph illustrating the rise in the percentage of unmarried mothers since World War II.

◀ Gay relationships have become more accepted in society since World War II and there are gay communities in many cities.

▶ A family celebrate Christmas in 1955. Fewer presents were given than is usually the case today.

1948
"Baby boom" – high number of births after the war.

1950s
"A" and "O" levels introduced.

1961
Contraceptive pill available.

1965
First comprehensive schools set up.

1967
Homosexuality no longer against the law.

1980s
Britain's divorce rate is the highest in Europe.

1986
Corporal punishment banned in state schools.

1991
SATs introduced.

2005
Civil partnerships for same sex couples.

2012
Half of all babies predicted to be born to unmarried mothers if present trends continue.

CHILDREN AND FAMILIES

In some ways, by the end of the 20th century children were better looked after than ever before. They had more toys, more clothes and were more likely to have their own room. There was a greater awareness of problems such as bullying and child abuse, and it was no longer legal for parents or teachers to hit children. Before the 1960s, the cane swished regularly in most schools. Not everything had changed for the better, however.

HAPPIER?

Some people said that the 1940s were the happiest times of their lives because, although they had little money, people were friendlier and helped each other more. At the same time, however, many couples that no longer loved each other were trapped in marriage. By the 1990s, we were freer to do what we wanted. We had more "rights". But this could increase family breakdown, leaving children feeling insecure and even unwanted.

THEN AND NOW

Before the 1960s, children were punished by being beaten with canes, shoes, rulers and belts on the hand or the bottom. By the 1980s, the normal school punishment was a telling off, detention or suspension.

Since at least the 18th century, women had been arguing for equal treatment with men. They made some gains, such as the right to vote for women over 30 in 1918, before World War II. But it was between 1945 and 2006 that they really began to win equality.

WOMEN'S LIB

The campaign for "liberation" (freedom) of British women began around 1970. Its most famous leader was the writer Germaine Greer (left). "Why shouldn't men do the ironing and women cut the grass?" she argued. Laws were passed in 1970 and 1975 saying women had to be treated the same as men and earn the same money for the same work.

> **"** *My mother was a physiotherapist. After the war she had two children, me and my brother, but she didn't stop work. That was very unusual in those days. When I told one of my friends at school, he said, 'You've got a funny mum!'* **"**
>
> **James Graham, remembering his family in the 1950s and 60s**

Some members of the "women's lib" movement wanted the language to be changed. Expressions such as "mankind" meaning "the human race" were wrong, they claimed – some even objected to "manhole cover". Starting in the late 1960s, the women's movement began to alter British thinking.

NEW WOMEN

Women were given jobs that only men had done previously. They became judges, army officers and surgeons. In 1979, Margaret Thatcher became the country's first female prime minister.

◄ A girl models one of the symbols of the 1960s – the mini skirt.

BUZZ BOX

Women saw daring mini skirts as a badge of their new freedom. It showed that they were doing what they wanted, not what their parents and elders wanted.

▲ Despite advances in sexual equality, today the great majority of the world's leaders are still men.

Girls began to do better than boys at school and went on to well-paid careers. By the 1980s, some men were choosing to stay at home as "house husbands" while their better-paid partners went out to work. This was rare, though, and the new life of juggling work and children and home put women under a lot of stress.

GLASS CEILING

By 2000, women were supposed to be fully equal to men. However, despite making great advances, there were still few women in key positions, such as managing large companies. This was explained by the phrase "glass ceiling". This meant that men put up an invisible barrier stopping women getting to the very top jobs that had traditionally been done by men.

In 1945, less than 25 per cent of university students were women. By 2006 their numbers had doubled to over 50 per cent.

▶ In 1979 Margaret Thatcher became Britain's first female prime minister.

TIMELINE

1961
Contraceptive pill available.

1969-1971
Divorce made less complicated.

Women's liberation march in London

1975
Law passed ensuring equal pay for men and women doing the same work.

1979
Margaret Thatcher becomes Britain's first female prime minister.

1994
Women priests in Church of England.

2004
Dame Brenda Hale becomes Britain's first female law lord.

2006
Work and Families Act introduces nine months maternity leave and two weeks paternity leave.

On average British people were living about ten years longer in 2000 than they had in 1950. There were many reasons for this, but one of the most important was the setting up of the National Health Service (NHS) in 1948.

HEALTH FOR ALL

At the end of World War II, the Labour Government introduced sweeping social reforms known as the Welfare State. These reforms gave everyone access to free healthcare, education and social care. The aim of the NHS was to give everyone healthcare when they needed it, paid for through taxes. For the first time ever, all British people had a doctor and a dentist, and everyone could go into hospital when they needed to.

At the same time, new treatments were being discovered for diseases that had been killers. Antibiotics dealt with tuberculosis, for instance, and a vaccination was found against polio. During the 1960s, a link between cigarettes and cancer was shown, encouraging smokers to quit.

> *The NHS will place this country in the forefront of all countries of the world in medical services ... It will keep very many people alive who might otherwise be dead. It will relieve suffering ... It will be a great contribution towards the wellbeing of the common people of Great Britain.*

Aneurin Bevan introducing the NHS to the House of Commons, 1946

HIGH COSTS

Sadly, these wonderful developments brought fresh problems. New medicines and treatments were terribly expensive, so the cost of the NHS soared. As people lived longer, more money was needed for state pensions (introduced in 1946), housing and health treatment. To find this money, the government started charging NHS patients. It began with small charges for dentistry and medicines. These gradually increased, and there were new charges for things

BUZZ BOX

Before the NHS, patients paid their doctors, so those with rich patients became very wealthy. Under the NHS, doctors were paid according to the number of patients they had – so some earned far less.

◀ A scene in a hospital's baby ward in 1949. The NHS had been running just a year by the time this picture was taken.

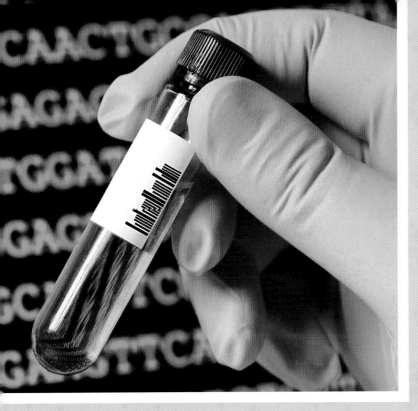

The cost of medicines has increased enormously since the NHS was set up in 1948.

like eye tests and spectacles in 1988. Long waiting lists developed for some operations. As a result, some better-off patients chose to pay for private care – just as they had done before the NHS.

NEW PROBLEMS

There were deadly new diseases, too, like HIV-AIDS. Our diet also became more unhealthy, as we began to eat more fatty foods. By the 21st century, the nation was gripped by a wave of obesity that brought with it health problems such as heart disease and cancer. By 2007, nearly a quarter of all adults in Britain were clinically obese.

◄ The popularity of fatty foods such as chips, together with a less active lifestyle, has meant that many of us have got fatter.

TIMELINE

1948
NHS set up.

1952
Dental charges introduced.

1955
New polio vaccine discovered.

1960
First hip replacement operation.

1971
Health warnings appear on cigarette packets.

1978
AIDS worries build.

1983
First successful heart and lung transplant.

2007
Smoking in public places banned.

THEN AND NOW

Forty years ago, when people's hip joints wore out they were often unable to walk. Today surgeons give patients new, artificial hips made of metal and plastic.

21

MIXING TOGETHER

From the earliest times, Britain has welcomed settlers from overseas. This has happened since 1945, too, with millions of new immigrants from all corners of the globe. They have changed the appearance and behaviour of British society in many ways.

IMMIGRATION

After World War II, many Europeans came to Britain to start new lives. From 1948, thousands more immigrants arrived from the Caribbean, India and Pakistan. They were needed because there were not enough working people in Britain. The NHS, particularly short of doctors and nurses, was kept going by skilled workers from overseas. The immigrants brought their customs and traditions with them. From the Caribbean came a new style of music and a love of sport. Pakistanis were often Muslims, which led to

▼ The arrival of people from other cultures in Britain has changed many things, including our diet. Curry is now Britain's favourite dish.

▲ Immigrants from the Caribbean arrive in London in 1950.

Britain getting its first mosques. Perhaps the most noticeable change was in food, especially curries from India. Spicy dishes like tikka and tandoori were almost unknown in 1945. By 1995 they had become the nation's favourite. In 2004, a fresh wave of immigrants came, this time from Poland and other East European countries that had gained membership of the European Union (EU).

THEN AND NOW

In 1945, just about all school pupils were white and spoke English at home. By 2005, in some British schools nearly all the pupils were non-white and did not speak English fluently .

▲ British now! This couple are taking part in a citizenship ceremony in Bradford, 2005.

1948
Immigration from Britain's former colonies begins as the ship *Empire Windrush* brings settlers from the Caribbean.

1965
First of several laws passed to make racial discrimination illegal.

1981
Race riots in Brixton, London.

2000s
New wave of immigrants from Eastern Europe.

2002
Paul Boateng becomes Britain's first black cabinet minister. Rabinder Singh becomes Britain's first Sikh judge the next year.

MULTICULTURAL?

Immigration produced difficulties. Some British people felt that their jobs and way of life was being taken over by "outsiders". This led to riots in cities like London and Bradford. New laws were introduced from 1965 onwards to make it illegal to discriminate against someone because of their race or colour. A huge effort was made to create a multicultural nation where many different ways of life mixed together.

NEW UNITY

In the 21st century, the government changed its mind about multi-culturalism. It was worried that the policy was making lots of little separate communities instead of holding the country together. The new idea was to stress our common culture, values and history. Citizenship ceremonies were introduced to make sure immigrants were given an idea of British values and culture.

▼ A mosque in Bradford, Yorkshire.

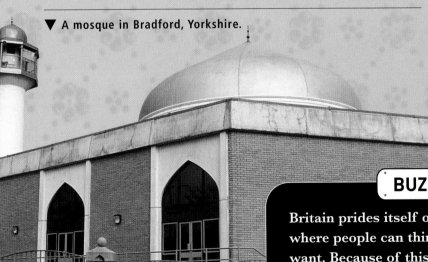

BUZZ BOX

Britain prides itself on being a free country where people can think and say what they want. Because of this, it has given asylum to immigrants fleeing countries where they are in danger because of their beliefs.

FAR AND WIDE

Wealth and technology allow us to travel far more often and more easily than our parents and grandparents. For example, in 1945, going to Australia was a journey of a lifetime. Today people fly there just for a holiday!

▲ Traffic free! The M1 when it opened in 1959.

▲ In contrast, Britain's motorways today are often choked with traffic.

ON THE ROAD

Before 1950, a car was a luxury. Most short journeys were made on foot – it was quite normal to walk a mile or two to work – or cycle. For longer journeys there were buses and trains. Flying was only for the wealthy. Many families did not often travel outside the district where they lived and worked, except for an annual holiday by the seaside.

By the late 1960s, there were four times as many cars as there were in 1950. Railways were being closed and motorways opened. Young people, who were better off than ever before, could drive a motor scooter or a motorbike at the age of 16. Thirty years later, almost three-quarters of all households had a car. Car ownership changed lives. Supermarkets moved to locations outside town centres. Driving to work, often many miles, became common. Children were taken to clubs and activities far from their home. Dating couples could get away from the eyes of their parents and neighbours.

> **"***Going to see my cousins in Yorkshire was a great adventure in the 1950s. 320 miles took all day, from breakfast to dark. Dad always took a spare fan belt and other bits and pieces in case the car broke down.***"**
>
> Charlie Ramsbotham, personal interview with the author, 2007

When motorways were first opened, there were no speed limits. Racing drivers testing their cars at night reached speeds of 185 mph! Nowadays the maximum legal speed permitted is 70 mph.

▲ Cheap flights allow many families to travel all over the world.

ACCIDENTS

Cars brought freedom – and tragedy. By the 1960s, thousands of people were killed on the roads ever year. To deal with this, new safety measures were introduced. Motorcyclists had to wear crash helmets and car drivers seat belts, and MOT tests were compulsory for all vehicles. Strict drink-driving limits were also introduced.

TAKING TO THE SKIES

Cheap flights allowed most working families to take sunshine holidays in places that only the rich visited in the 1950s. By the 21st century, groups were going to European cities for birthday parties and other special occasions. Some people even went to New York to do their shopping!

▲ Cars now have to undergo annual MOT tests to make sure they are roadworthy.

TIMELINE

1950
First cheap package holidays go on sale.

1958
First motorway opened.

1959
"Mini" car goes on sale for £499.

1994
Channel Tunnel opens.

2007
Calls for air travel to be limited to cut pollution.

BUZZ BOX

In the 1960s, teenagers joined gangs of Mods or Rockers. The Mods drove scooters and wore trendy clothes. The leather-wearing Rockers drove motorbikes.

A young person from 21st-century Britain taken back to the 1940s might be very bored: no TV, no computer games, no mobile phones! But children then were no more bored than they are today, they just had different amusements.

◀ During the 1940s, when you wanted to make a telephone call you had to speak to an operator first. They then put your call through for you.

66 *Ah for those far off 50s! I remember rushing home from school to watch Billy Bunter, Mister Pastry, The Lone Ranger & The Cisco Kid and The Adventures of Robin Hood.* 99

Harley Jones remembers his 1950s childhood

▼ Today's youth can spend their leisure time listening to music on Ipods, playing computer games and much more.

VINYL WORLD

In the late 1940s, adults had less leisure time than in the 21st century. Hours of work were longer and the daily housework took ages. In their free time people listened to the wireless (radio), played cards or board games, did jigsaws, sang, listened to records or just chatted together. Children were used to playing outdoors in the street or fields.

Most homes got their first black-and-white TV set during the 1950s. This changed family life quite quickly. By the 60s, it was normal for the whole family to sit down to watch a popular TV programme – there were only two stations, BBC or ITV. For the young – now known as "teenagers" –

▲ To avoid an obesity epidemic, events such as fun runs were organised.

In the 1940s and 50s music was recorded on plastic discs. Then came cassette tapes in the 70s, CDs in the 80s, and digital recordings on personal stereos in the 2000s. What next?

there were also dances, youth clubs, juke boxes in milk bars (trendy cafes serving milk and milkshakes) and vinyl singles to collect.

SO MUCH MORE

Unofficial "pirate" radio stations began broadcasting in the 1960s. During the 1970s, Britain got colour TV and BBC2, and radio became even more varied. The 1980s saw even greater changes with cable and satellite TV and all kinds of other electronic gadgets such as computers and games consoles becoming available.

COUCH POTATOES

By the 1990s, doctors were becoming worried about the health of a nation that spent so much time sitting down to watch, play or listen. This led to a new interest in exercise of all kinds, and people were encouraged to keep fit. Fun runs were organised. It became fashionable to join a gym and more school time was given to sports and outdoor games.

BUZZ BOX

In 1966, 32.3 million watched England win the football World Cup, the country's biggest ever TV audience. This is even more amazing because only 15 million households had a TV in 1966 (compared with 24 million today).

TIMELINE

1950s
Pop music begins.

1952
First portable radio.

1955
ITV begins broadcasting.

1963
The Beatles top the charts for the first time.

1978
First PC on sale.

1979
First personal stereo on sale.

1982
First CDs on sale.

1985
First mobile phone on sale.

1990
First laptop.

1991
World Wide Web available for all.

2005
Britain wins right to host 2012 Olympics.

GLOSSARY

affluence	wealth
asylum	protection from danger
consumer	anyone who buys things
currency	the type of money a country uses
decimal	modern system of currency, where money is divided up into pounds and pence
enamel	hard, non-rusting coating on metal
habitation	living place
immigrant	person who enters another country to live there
inflation	rising prices
juke box	machine for playing records in a public place
laminate	hard plastic surface
laundrette	building where people can go to do their washing
linoleum	hard plastic flooring
mangle	hand-operated machine for squeezing the water out of wet clothes
multicultural	mixing many cultures together
NHS	National Health Service
obese	seriously overweight
perish	go rotten, die
pirate radio	illegal radio station broadcasting from a ship off the coast
porcelain	china
privy	outside, non-flushing toilet
processed	manufactured
rationing	making sure everyone gets their fair share of important or luxury foods and goods
slum	housing unfit for living in
Tax	Money deducted from earnings by the government, which is then used to pay for public services
tuberculosis	killer lung disease
unemployed	out of work
vaccination	means of protecting a person against a disease

FURTHER INFORMATION
Books to read

For teachers
Arthur Marwick, British Society Since 1945, Penguin, 2003

Kenneth O. Morgan, Britain Since 1945, Oxford, 2001

For pupils
Stewart Ross, Britain Since 1930, Evans, 2003

Sally Hewitt, The 1970s (I Can remember), Franklin Watts, 2003

Jane Shuter, Britain Since 1930, Heinemann, 2005

Websites
http://www.bbc.co.uk/history/british/modern/overview_1945_present_01

http://www.ageconcern.org.uk/TimeCapsule/1950s_D8A72E0B8C8641E6922CABF70
7CE7747 (and follow links to time capsules)

http://www.great-britain.co.uk/history/post45.htm

http://www.historylearningsite.co.uk/medical_changes_from_1945

http://www.inthe80s.com/timeline

http://www.bbc.co.uk/wales/southeast/sites/newport/pages/article_prefabs

Places to visit
http://www.southbanklondon.com	The South Bank, London
htttp://www.beatlesstory.com	The Beatles Story, Liverpool
http://www.museumoflondon.org.uk	Museum of London, London
http://www.vam.ac.uk	Victoria and Albert Museum, London
http://www.transport-museum.com	Coventry Transport Museum

Note to parents and teachers: Every effort has been made by the Publishers to ensure that these websites are suitable for children, that they are of the highest educational value, and that they contain no inappropriate or offensive material. However, because of the nature of the Internet, it is impossible to guarantee that the contents of these sites will not be altered. We strongly advise that Internet access is supervised by a responsible adult.